the complete
HANDWRITING
PRACTICE
WORKBOOK

for kids

Email us at
modernkidpress@gmail.com
to get free extras!

Just title the email "Handwriting Practice"
and we will send some extra
surprises your way!

THE COMPLETE HANDWRITING PRACTICE WORKBOOK

THIS BOOK BELONGS TO

Name

Contents

PART 1: Letters.....................5

PART 2: Words.....................59

PART 3: Numbers.....................87

PART 4: Sentences...................99

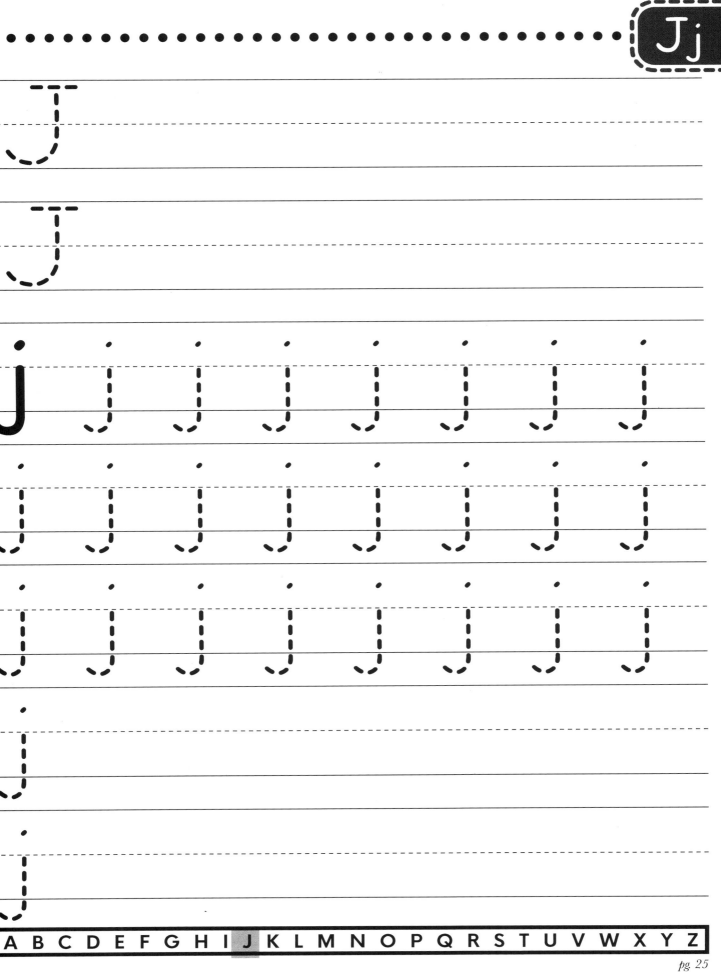

K is for koala

Trace each letter then write it on your own. ✏️

K K K K K K

K K K K K K

K K K K K K

A B C D E F G H I J **K** L M N O P Q R S T U V W X Y Z

A B C D E F G H I J K L M N O P Q R S T U V W X Y Z

L is for lobster

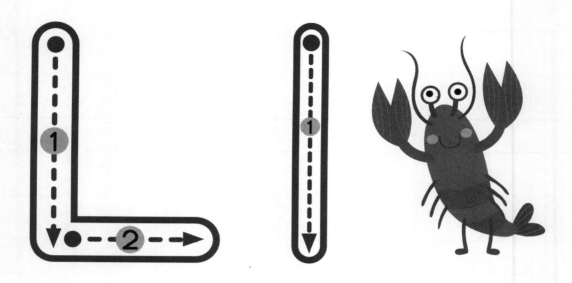

Trace each letter then write it on your own.

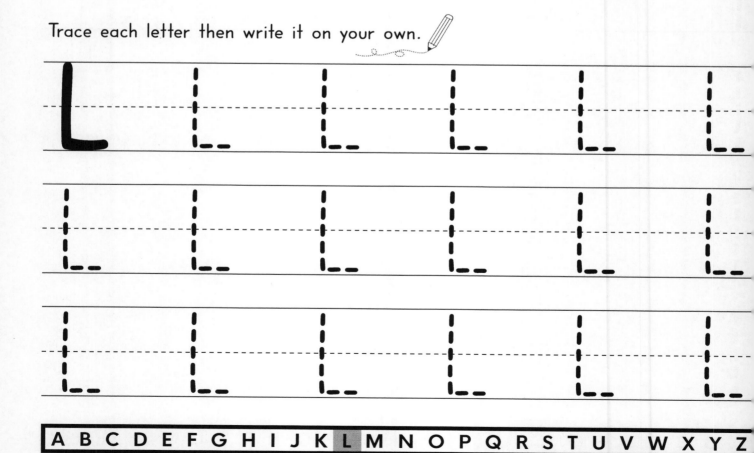

A B C D E F G H I J K L M N O P Q R S T U V W X Y Z

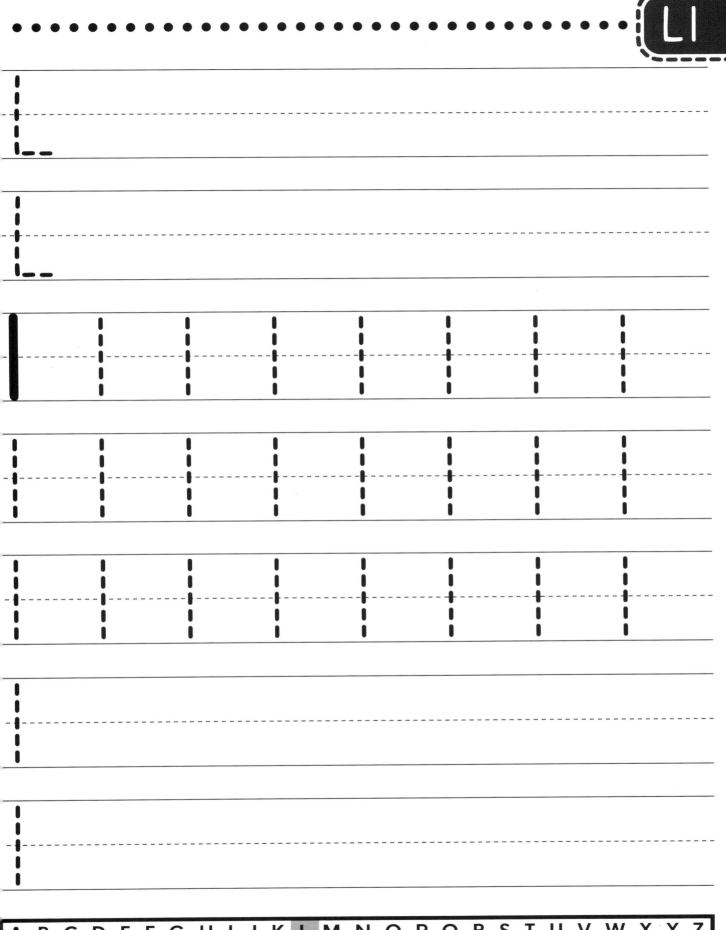

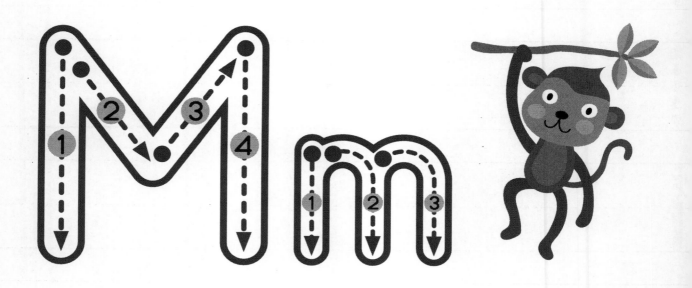

Trace each letter then write it on your own.

M M M M M

M M M M

M M M M

A B C D E F G H I J K L M N O P Q R S T U V W X Y Z

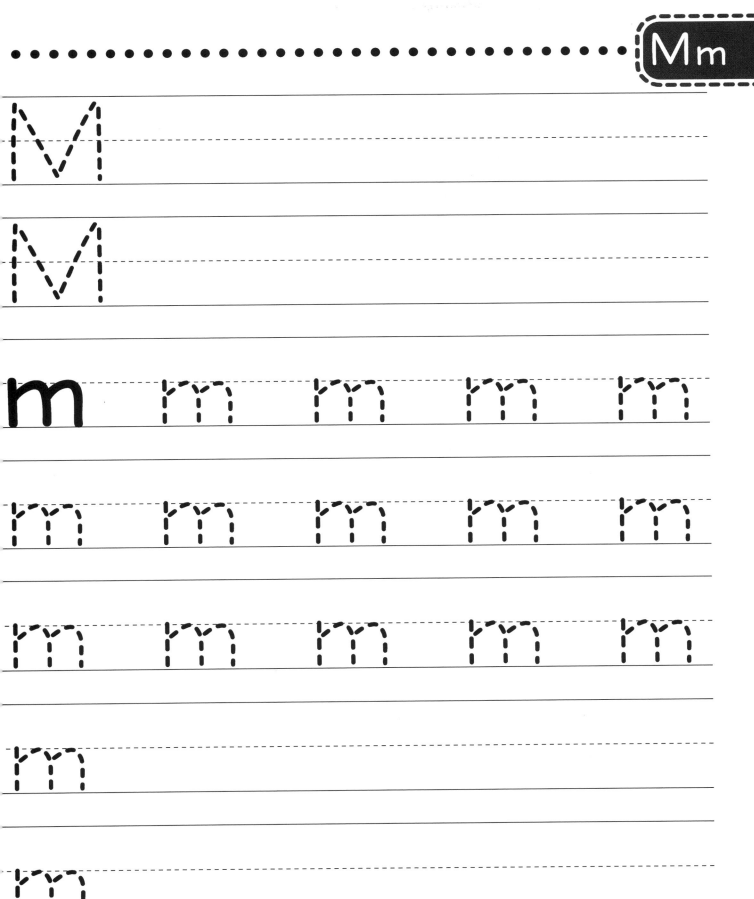

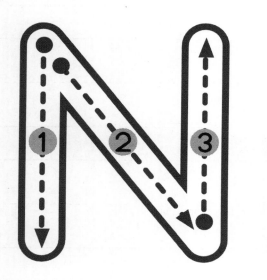  

Trace each letter then write it on your own.

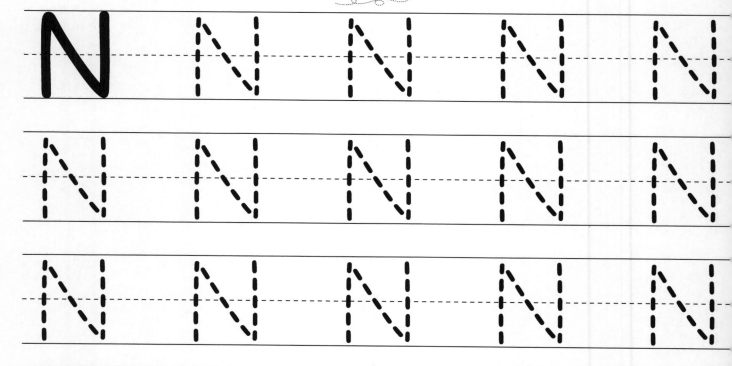

A B C D E F G H I J K L M **N** O P Q R S T U V W X Y Z

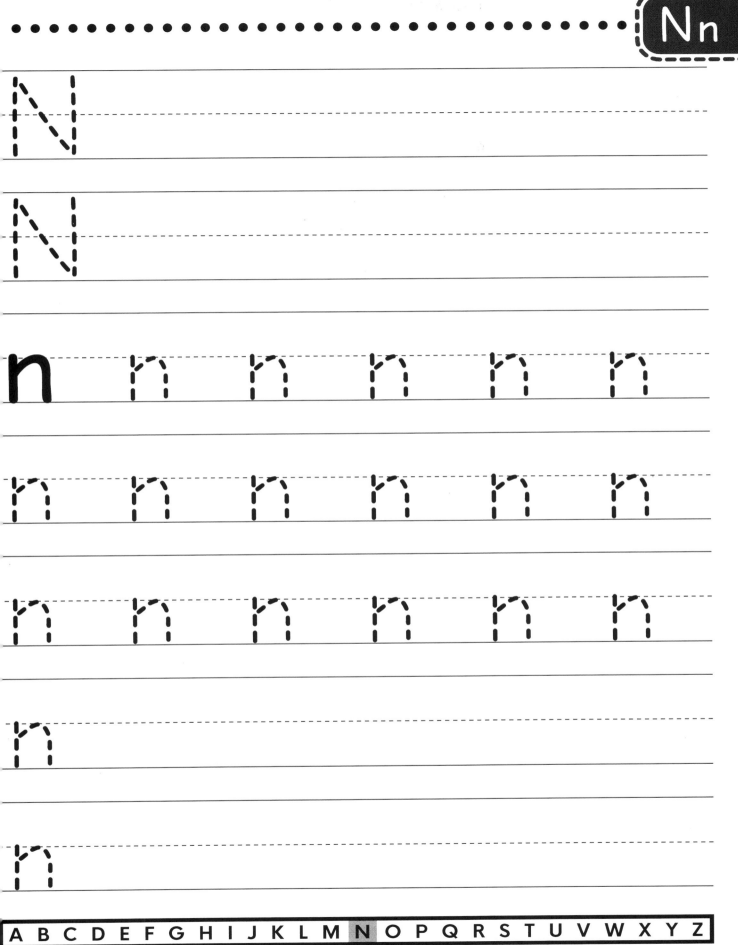

ABCDEFGHIJKLMN OPQRSTUVWXYZ

O is for oyster

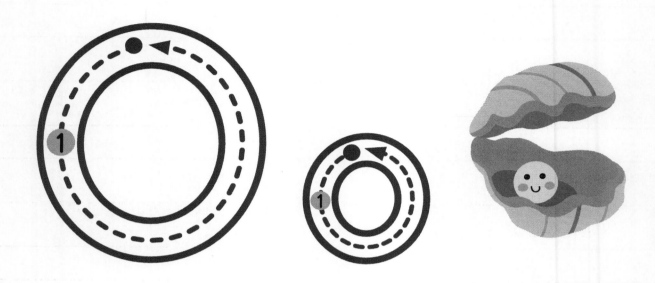

Trace each letter then write it on your own.

A B C D E F G H I J K L M N O P Q R S T U V W X Y Z

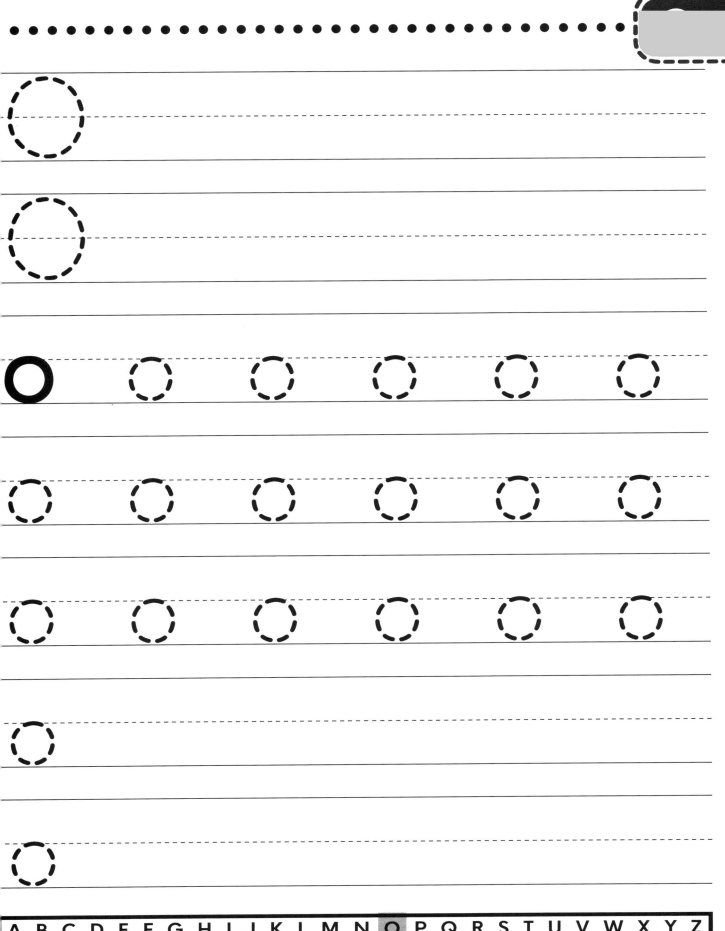

ABCDEFGHIJKLMN**O**PQRSTUVWXYZ

P is for pirate

Trace each letter then write it on your own. ✏️

P P P P P

P P P P P

P P P P P

A B C D E F G H I J K L M N O P Q R S T U V W X Y Z

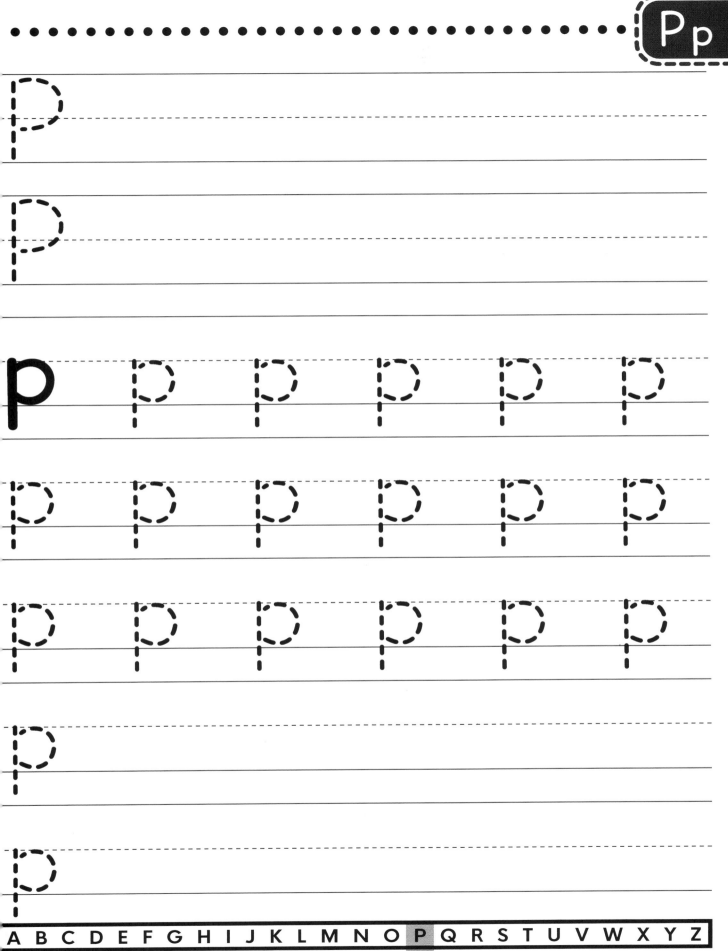

A B C D E F G H I J K L M N O P Q R S T U V W X Y Z

Q is for queen

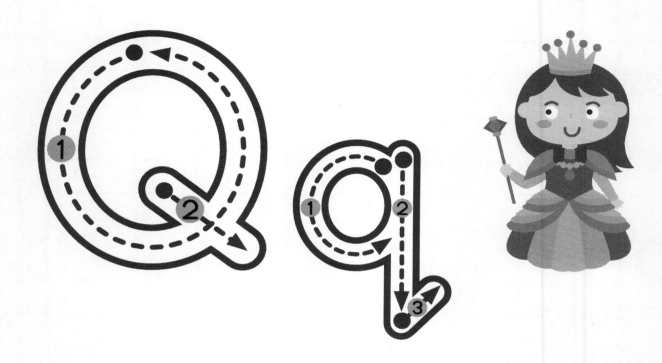

Trace each letter then write it on your own.

Q   Q   Q   Q

Q   Q   Q   Q

Q   Q   Q   Q

A B C D E F G H I J K L M N O P Q R S T U V W X Y Z

S

S

S S S S S S S

S S S S S S S

S S S S S S S

S

S

A B C D E F G H I J K L M N O P Q R S T U V W X Y Z

T is for toucan

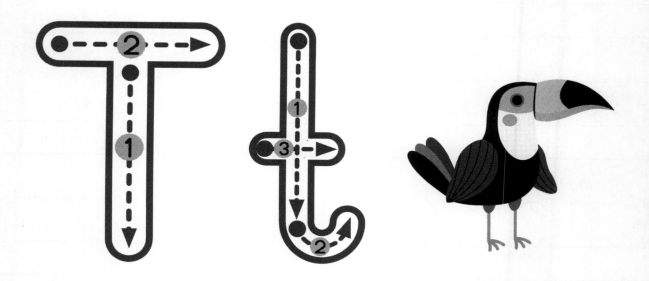

Trace each letter then write it on your own.

T ─T─ ─T─ ─T─ ─T─

─T─ ─T─ ─T─ ─T─ ─T─

─T─ ─T─ ─T─ ─T─ ─T─

A B C D E F G H I J K L M N O P Q R S T U V W X Y Z

U is for umbrella

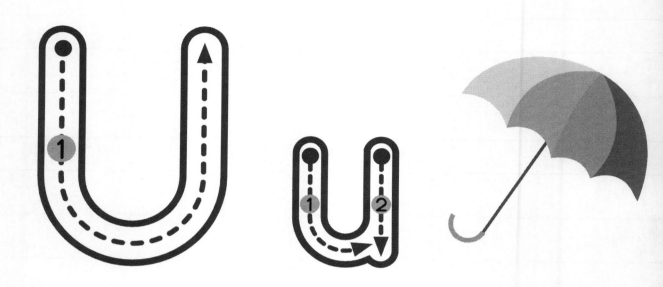

Trace each letter then write it on your own.

U U U U U

U U U U U

U U U U U

A B C D E F G H I J K L M N O P Q R S T U V W X Y Z

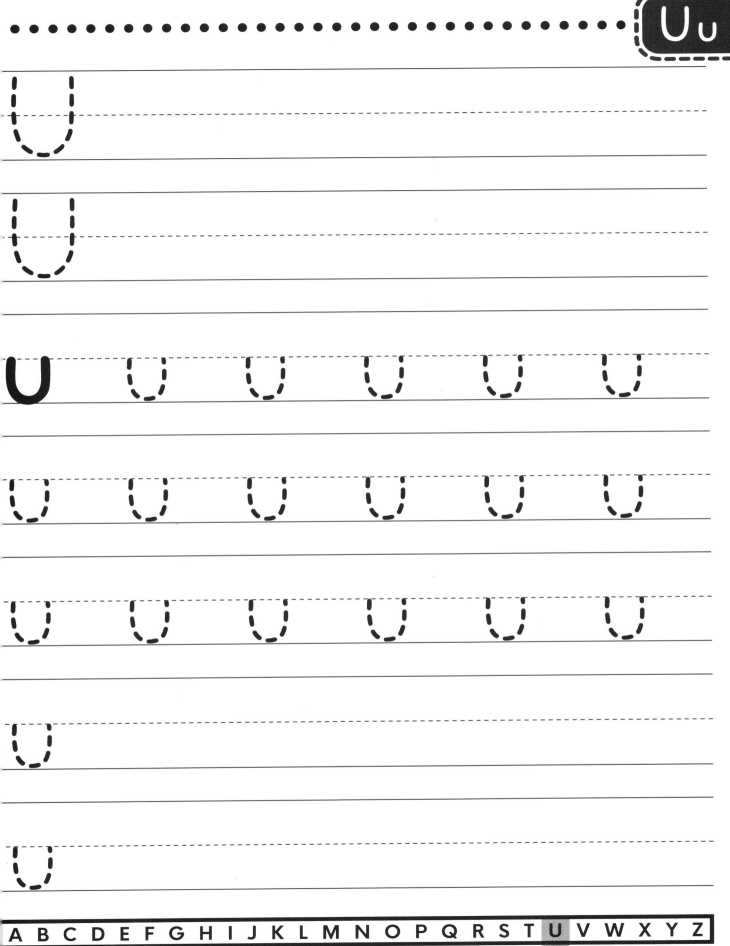

V is for violin

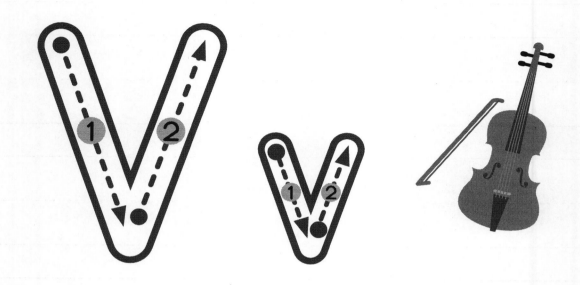

Trace each letter then write it on your own.

V V V V V V V

V V V V V

V V V V V

A B C D E F G H I J K L M N O P Q R S T U V W X Y Z

W is for whale

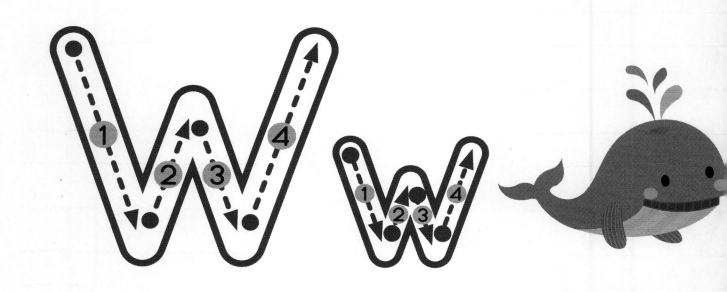

Trace each letter then write it on your own.

W W W W W W W

W W W W W W W

W W W W W W W

A B C D E F G H I J K L M N O P Q R S T U V **W** X Y Z

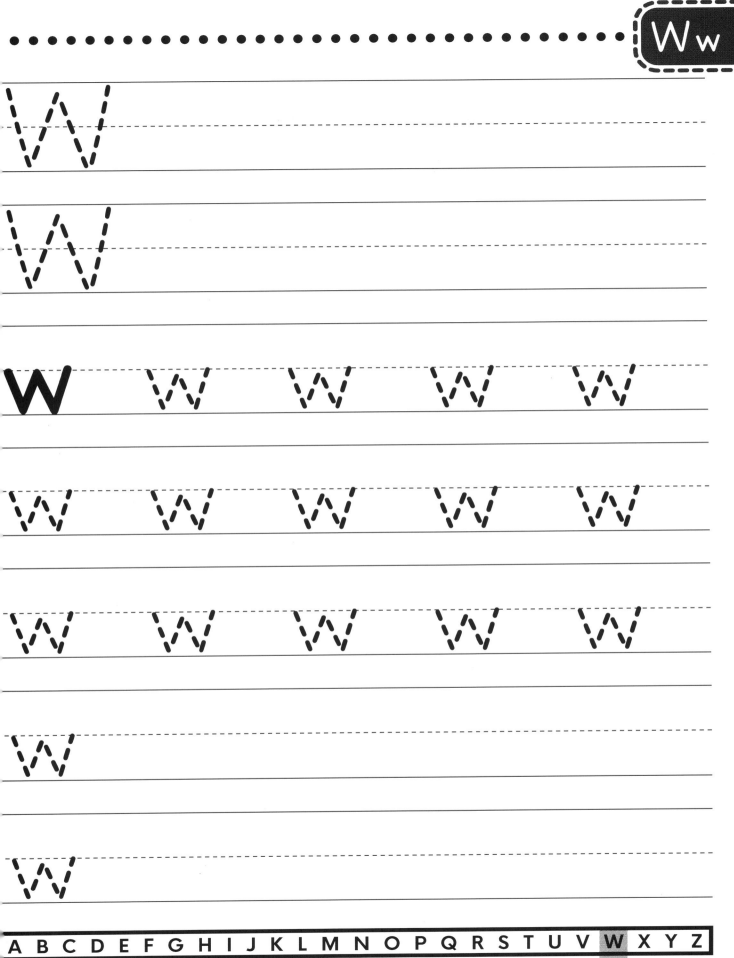

X is for x-ray

Trace each letter then write it on your own.

X X X X X

X X X X

X X X X

A B C D E F G H I J K L M N O P Q R S T U V W X Y Z

Y is for yak

Trace each letter then write it on your own.

Y   Y   Y   Y   Y

Y   Y   Y   Y   Y

Y   Y   Y   Y   Y

A B C D E F G H I J K L M N O P Q R S T U V W X Y Z

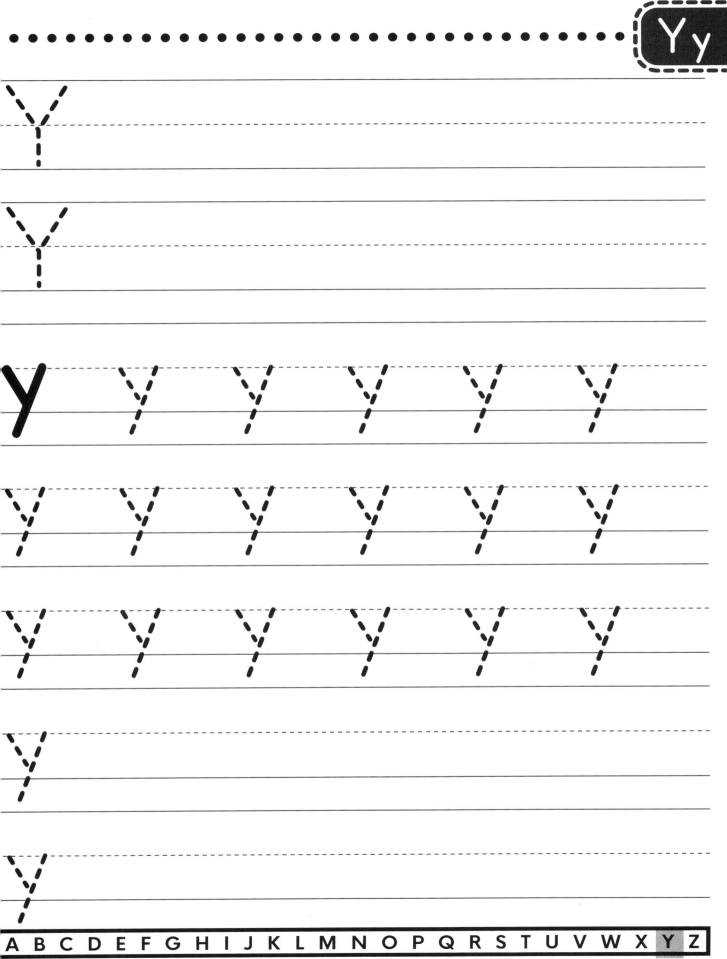

A B C D E F G H I J K L M N O P Q R S T U V W X Y Z

Z is for zipper

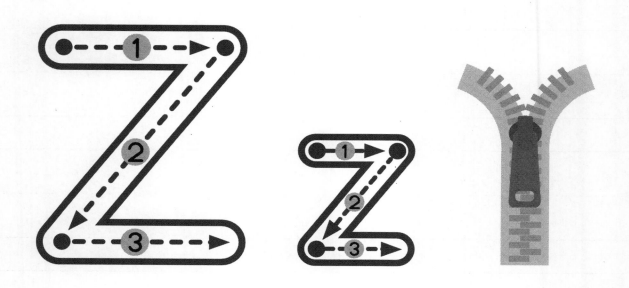

Trace each letter then write it on your own. ✏

Z Z Z Z Z

Z Z Z Z Z

Z Z Z Z Z

A B C D E F G H I J K L M N O P Q R S T U V W X Y **Z**

Z z

Z

Z

Z   Z   Z   Z   Z   Z

Z   Z   Z   Z   Z   Z

Z   Z   Z   Z   Z   Z

Z

Z

A B C D E F G H I J K L M N O P Q R S T U V W X Y Z

pg 57

Way to go, you made it through the whole alphabet!
Now let's try tracing it altogether.

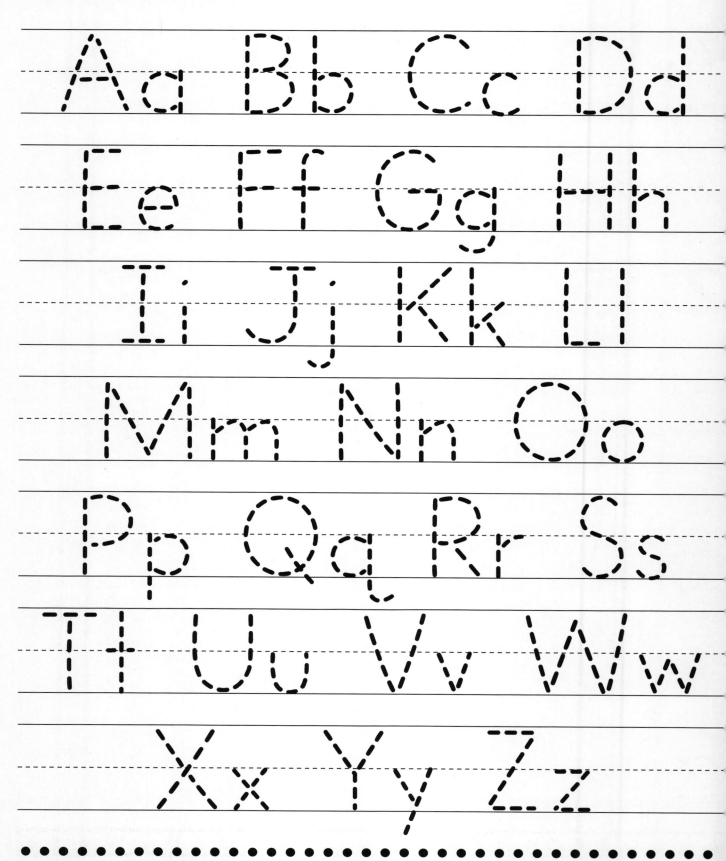

PART 2

WORDS

Way to tackle that alphabet! You look ready to put those letters together to form words. We are going to start with the letter 'A' and work our way through the alphabet once more so grab your pencil and let's get started!

Trace each word then write it on your own.

am am am

and   and   and

away away

Trace each word then write it on your own.

be   be   be   be

blue   blue   blue

big   big   big

Trace each word then write it on your own.

can   can   can

come   come

could   could

ace each word then write it on your own.

do   do   do   do

did   did   did

does   does

A B C D E F G H I J K L M N O P Q R S T U V W X Y Z

Trace each word then write it on your own.

eat   eat   eat

each   each

ever   ever   eve|

race each word then write it on your own.

find find find

for for for

funny funny

A B C D E **F** G H I J K L M N O P Q R S T U V W X Y Z

Trace each word then write it on your own.

go go go go

get get get

good good

A B C D E F **G** H I J K L M N O P Q R S T U V W X Y :

ace each word then write it on your own.

had had had

here here

help help help

A B C D E F G **H** I J K L M N O P Q R S T U V W X Y Z

Trace each word then write it on your own.

in in in in in

is is is is is

into into into

| A | B | C | D | E | F | G | H | I | J | K | L | M | N | O | P | Q | R | S | T | U | V | W | X | Y |

race each word then write it on your own.

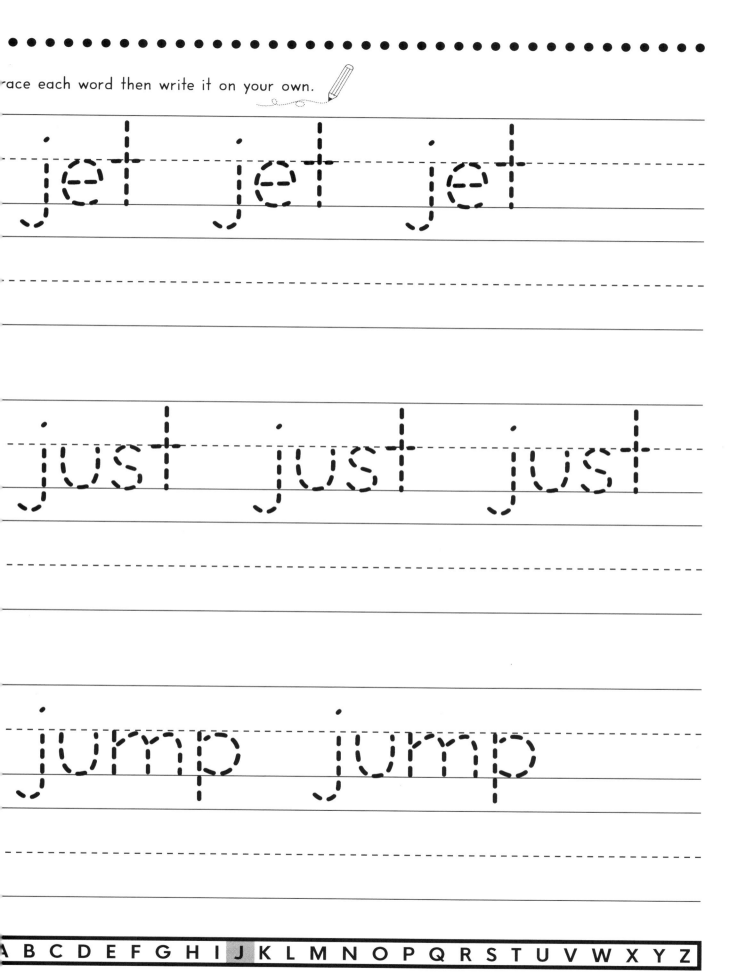

jet jet jet

just just just

jump jump

A B C D E F G H I J K L M N O P Q R S T U V W X Y Z

Trace each word then write it on your own. ✏️

know know

kite kite kite

key key key

A B C D E F G H I J K L M N O P Q R S T U V W X Y

race each word then write it on your own.

like   like   like

ook   look   look

ittle   little

Trace each word then write it on your own.

make make make

me me me

my my my

A B C D E F G H I J K L **M** N O P Q R S T U V W X Y

race each word then write it on your own.

now now now

new new new

no no no

A B C D E F G H I J K L M N O P Q R S T U V W X Y Z

Trace each word then write it on your own.

on   on   on   on

out   out   out

old   old   old

race each word then write it on your own.

put put put

play play play

park park

A B C D E F G H I J K L M N O P Q R S T U V W X Y Z

Trace each word then write it on your own.

quit   quit   quit

quiet   quiet

queen   queen

A B C D E F G H I J K L M N O P Q R S T U V W X Y

race each word then write it on your own.

red   red   red

run   run   run

ride   ride   ride

A B C D E F G H I J K L M N O P Q R S T U V W X Y Z

Trace each word then write it on your own.

so so so so

see see see

said said said

A B C D E F G H I J K L M N O P Q R **S** T U V W X Y

race each word then write it on your own.

to to to to

the the the the

this this this this

A B C D E F G H I J K L M N O P Q R S T U V W X Y Z

Trace each word then write it on your own.

up up up up

use use use

under under

A B C D E F G H I J K L M N O P Q R S T **U** V W X Y

very   very   very

visit   visit   visit

van   van   van

| A | B | C | D | E | F | G | H | I | J | K | L | M | N | O | P | Q | R | S | T | U | V | W | X | Y | Z |

Trace each word then write it on your own.

we   we   we

was   was   was

where   where

A B C D E F G H I J K L M N O P Q R S T U V **W** X Y

ace each word then write it on your own.

x-ray   x-ray

xi   xi   xi   xi

xylophone

A B C D E F G H I J K L M N O P Q R S T U V W X Y Z

Trace each word then write it on your own.

you you you

yes yes yes

yellow yellow

A B C D E F G H I J K L M N O P Q R S T U V W X Y

race each word then write it on your own.

zip   zip   zip

zipper   zipper

zoo   zoo   zoo

A B C D E F G H I J K L M N O P Q R S T U V W X Y **Z**

Trace each word then write it on your own.

superb!

bravo!

awesome!

A B C D E F G H I J K L M N O P Q R S T U V W X Y

NUMBERS

Now that you have mastered writing words,
let's practice writing numbers 1 through 10!

Trace the number then write it on your own.

0   0   0   0

0

zero zero zero

zero

How many fish are there?
Write the number in the blank below.

There are _____ fish.

| 0 | 1 | 2 | 3 | 4 | 5 | 6 | 7 | 8 | 9 | 1 |

Trace the number then write it on your own.

I I I I I I I I I I

I

one one one

one

How many hedghogs are there?
Write the number in the blank below.

There are _____ hedghogs.

	1	2	3	4	5	6	7	8	9	1 0

Trace the number then write it on your own.

2 2 2 2 2

2

two two two

two

How many ice cream cones are there?
Write the number in the blank below.

There are _____ ice cream cones.

| 0 | 1 | 2 | 3 | 4 | 5 | 6 | 7 | 8 | 9 | 1 |

Trace the number then write it on your own.

3 ~3~ ~3~ ~3~ ~3~

~3~

three ~three~

~three~

How many trucks are there?
Write the number in the blank below.

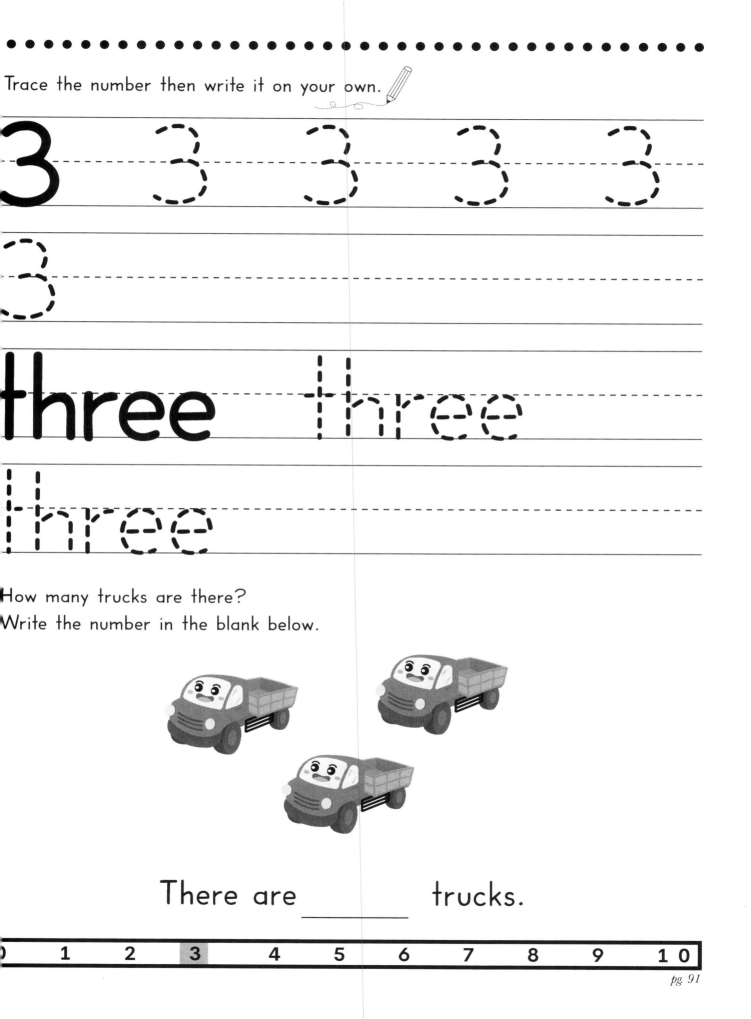

There are _____ trucks.

| 0 | 1 | 2 | 3 | 4 | 5 | 6 | 7 | 8 | 9 | 1 0 |

Trace the number then write it on your own.

4   4   4   4

4

four four four

four

How many lions are there?
Write the number in the blank below.

There are _____ lions.

0	1	2	3	4	5	6	7	8	9	1

Trace the number then write it on your own.

5 5 5 5 5

5

five five five

five

How many unicorns are there?
Write the number in the blank below.

There are _____ unicorns.

| 1 | 2 | 3 | 4 | 5 | 6 | 7 | 8 | 9 | 10 |

Trace the number then write it on your own.

6   6   6   6

6

six   six   six   six

six

How many sharks are there?
Write the number in the blank below.

There are _____ sharks.

| 0 | 1 | 2 | 3 | 4 | 5 | 6 | 7 | 8 | 9 | 1 |

Trace the number then write it on your own.

7   7   7   7   7

7

seven   seven

seven

How many rainbows are there?
Write the number in the blank below.

There are _____ rainbows.

| 1 | 2 | 3 | 4 | 5 | 6 | 7 | 8 | 9 | 1 0 |

Trace the number then write it on your own. ✏

8 8 8 8 8

8

eight   eight

eight

How many pigs are there?
Write the number in the blank below.

There are _____ pigs.

| 0 | 1 | 2 | 3 | 4 | 5 | 6 | 7 | 8 | 9 | 1 |

Trace the number then write it on your own.

q   q   q   q

q

nine   nine   nine

nine

How many robots are there?
Write the number in the blank below.

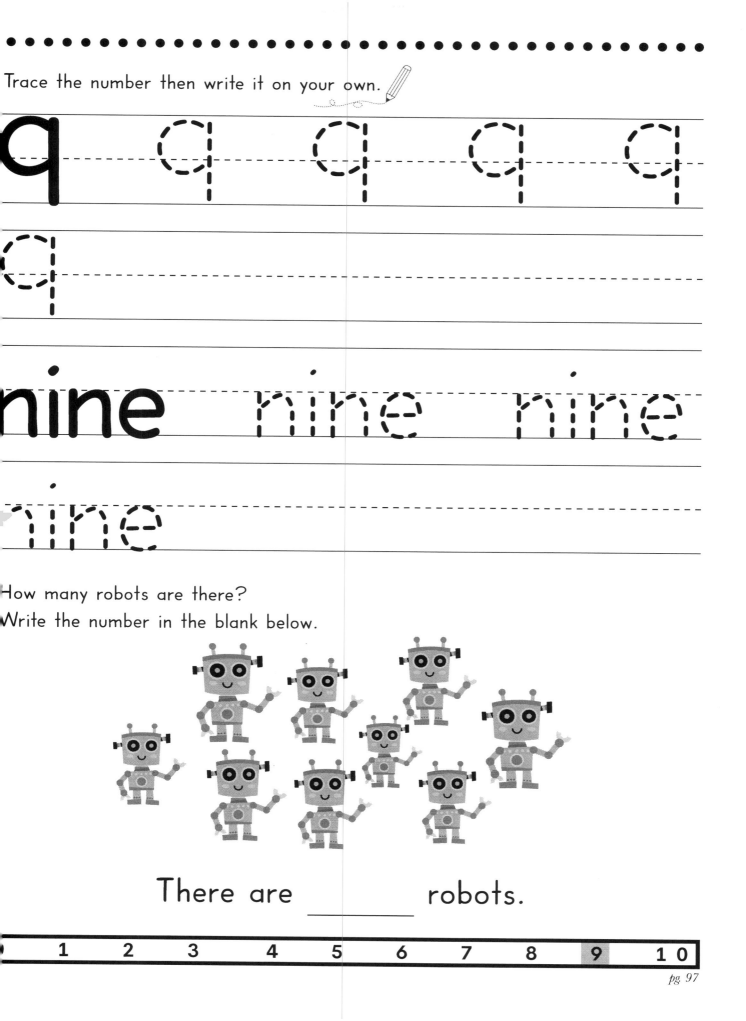

There are _____ robots.

| 1 | 2 | 3 | 4 | 5 | 6 | 7 | 8 | 9 | 1 0 |

Trace the number then write it on your own.

10   10   10   10

10

ten   ten   ten

ten

How many owls are there?
Write the number in the blank below.

There are _____ owls.

| 0 | 1 | 2 | 3 | 4 | 5 | 6 | 7 | 8 | 9 | 1 |

SENTENCES

In this section we are going to continue to build your muscle memory by stringing words into sentences! Keep up the good work!

Trace each sentence then write it on your own.

I like to play.

_____

_____

I fly my kite.

_____

_____

It goes up high

_____

_____

race each sentence then write it on your own.

Hal has a cat.

The cat sat.

I want a cat.

Trace each sentence then write it on your own.

Ed likes to dig.

He digs a lot.

Ed is my dog.

Here is my hat.

I wear my hat.

It is a good hat.

Trace each sentence then write it on your own.

I see a bus.

It is yellow.

The bus can go

ace each sentence then write it on your own.

My bike is red.

I like to ride.

I go fast.

Trace each sentence then write it on your own.

There is a bug.

I hug the bug.

He lives in a jug.

race each sentence then write it on your own.

I can walk.

I walk outside.

It is a nice day.

Trace each sentence then write it on your own.

The bird sings.

It sounds nice.

I sing too.

ace each sentence then write it on your own.

Look at the box.

What is in it?

It is a gift!

Trace each sentence then write it on your own.

The dog runs.

I run too.

We go fast.

Sal has a shell.

The shell is pink.

I want one too.

Trace each sentence then write it on your own.

This is my pup.

His name is Sir.

Sir likes to jump.

race each sentence then write it on your own.

I like to cut.

I cut the paper.

I cut and glue.

Trace each sentence then write it on your own.

The sun is hot.

I am hot too.

I go inside.

race each sentence then write it on your own.

The tent is blue.

It has a door.

I sleep in it.

Trace each sentence then write it on your own.

I love to bake.

I bake a cake.

Let's eat it!

Trace each sentence then write it on your own. ✏️

Ted is a clown.

He is funny.

We like to laugh.

Printed in Great Britain
by Amazon